Among Red Poppies in the Sand

Prose and Poetry
of Promise and Remembrance

My First Trip to Israel

Marcia Rome Levitz

BOOKSIDE Press

Copyright © 2023 by Marcia Rome Levitz

ISBN: 978-1-77883-047-1 (Paperback)

All rights reserved. No part of this publication may be reproduced, distributed, or transmitted in any form or by any means, including photocopying, recording, or other electronic or mechanical methods, without the prior written permission of the publisher, except in the case brief quotations embodied in critical reviews and other noncommercial uses permitted by copyright law.

The views expressed in this book are solely those of the author and do not necessarily reflect the views of the publisher, and the publisher hereby disclaims any responsibility for them. Some names and identifying details in this book have been changed to protect the privacy of individuals.

BookSide Press
877-741-8091
www.booksidepress.com
orders@booksidepress.com

Contents

Dedication..v
Origins..1
Shalom!..2
Operation Exodus...4
By Our Hand..6
Generation To Generation 8
The Sabbath 9
A Sabbath Blessing 10
Massada 11
A Child Is A Blessing 14
Eretz Israel...16
Awakening...18
What I Know Now..20
Epilogue 21

Dedication

I dedicate this book to my father, Howard William Rome, my mentor, my inspiration, who instilled in me the values by which I live, and who enabled me to open my heart and seek the meaning of what life could truly hold.

Origins

In my youth, <u>Anne Frank, The Diary of Anne Frank</u> intrigued me. I could not imagine the boredom she endured as a twelve-year-old hidden for two years in an attic. This book left an indelible image of a life lost and wasted… and why? Solely because she was a Jew.

When I held my son in my arms during his Berit Milah, I also held a clear understanding of my responsibilities as a Jewish mother.

As my responsibilities to my son lessened, I became involved with the United Jewish Federation of Northeastern New York, and I arranged young-leadership-development seminars for teaching, encouraging, and promoting, a better awareness of Jews in Israel and in the Diaspora.

This compilation of prose and poetry languished on my desk for several years, and finally I felt compelled to share it. My trip to Israel holds a special place in my memory and forever changed me.

Marcia Rome Levitz

Shalom!

This was my first trip to Israel, and accordingly, I was referred to as a first-timer throughout my visit. A large proportion of my traveling companions were first-timers, and I know now that it will not be my last homage.

The flight was long, more than ten hours; but as I watched the Tel Aviv sunrise washing the Mediterranean Sea with golden and red rays, and listened to the entire plane sing and clap to "Avenu ShalomAllechaim" I was rejuvenated. With a lump in my throat and tears in my eyes, I felt I had come home… Israel… the land of my forefathers, my heritage, our future. I could not believe I had come to this country at last.

As I deplaned and was awaiting my transportation to customs, I was fortunate to see Jews from around the world arriving as well: new Russian olim, a decorated Russian soldier and his ailing wife, two small boys who clung to their tired but overjoyed parents, an elderly woman with a gold tooth who spoke Yiddish with one of the participants, and a group of Ethiopian Jews. These are but a few of the many faces I remember that early morning, expressing the relief and excitement that I too experienced upon returning to our homeland.

Shalom! Shalom!
I have come home.
To the Promised Land
Where tall trees stand,
Planted by our hands,
Among red poppies in the sand.

Shalom! Shalom!
I have come home
Where faces inspire
An inner desire
To reach out a hand
To this Promised Land.

Shalom! Shalom!
We have come home;
To share with old friends
And new ones who lend
Their hearts and their souls;
Our destiny we hold.

Operation Exodus

Assimilation of immigrants into existing communities is fraught with difficulties as we Americans know all too well; but honoring an individual right to be free outweighs the problems both sides might have to address during this process. Language, customs, beliefs, economics, and even age are but a few of the multitude of problems these immigrants experience.

Operation Exodus was the vehicle by which many of the Jewish immigrants came to Israel. Fund-raising campaigns across this country are the primary instruments for the humanitarian and social services for Jews throughout the world.

In Israel the Jewish Agency directs campaign funds that help absorb, educate, and settle new immigrants, provide programs for disadvantaged youth, and care for the aged.

Operation Exodus was instituted for acquiring more monies to repatriate Jews from Russia and Ethiopia to Israel. Perhaps the same coordinated acquisition and distribution of funds should be employed in the cases of those Americans affected by September 11, 2001, disaster and those Afghans displaced into Pakistan and other areas of the world.

Tired faces, eyes with tears
Shed for joy, for they have come
Into the Promised Land.

A small boy takes his brother's hand
And 'round his mother's skirt he peers.
What lies ahead? Who knows the fear
He left behind or will face here?

A miracle is found on a bough in spring,
As these immigrants come
And with them bring
The hope, which all of us hold dear—
That freedom and the chance "to be"
Is God's blessing for thee and me.

Take heart, take part!
This miracle to be
Is for us who know,
And for them, is now!

Marcia Rome Levitz

By Our Hand

After the mitzvah of planting trees by our own hands in the Jewish National Forest, we ascended Mount Carmel via the Wadi Oren, formally the route taken by illegal immigrants returning to Israel from eastern Europe. We then headed to Haifa, a glorious seaport on the Mediterranean. We had a short but much needed night's rest, and in the morning we proceeded to Akko, the former British prison where Jewish underground members were incarcerated before 1948. Afterward, we traveled along the Purple Line, Israel's border with Lebanon. We were headed to the kibbutz Misgav Am.

This next poem is dedicated to the brave individuals who live at the border of Lebanon and Israel in the kibbutz Misgav Am, who endured a night of horror when terrorists held hostage the children's dormitory and, during that night, killed a two-and-one-half-year-old boy with the butt of a gun.

Misgav Am means "the desire of the people."

At the end of the world
There's hope on the hill'
Where the sweet smells of lilacs
And apple blossoms spill,
Where the laughter of children
Brings tears of joy,
Where the desires of the people
Share the memory of a boy.

Marcia Rome Levitz

Generation To Generation

Dinner that night was on a boat that departed Tiberias on Lake Kinneret. This was a beautiful and relaxing way to spend an evening with our thoughts after what we had learned that day.

Ascending into the Golan Heights in military jeeps driven by armed soldiers of the IDF, we traveled across beautiful desert-like terrain to visit the archaeological excavations of the oldest synagogue in Israel, Bat Ya'Ar.

The following day we visited an Israel Defense Force Army base and met with the commander of the world's best tank. He was nineteen-year-old Yoni, a poised and articulate man who said it all…he was there protecting this ex-Syrian stronghold because he could look down in the valley and see a small village. He pointed to the village and said, "I can see my parent's home, and I am here to protect them."

The Sabbath

That evening I ascended the slopes of the Judean hills and continued on into Jerusalem. As I entered the city, again a lump arose in my throat as I recited the She-hecheyanu, a prayer that gives praise to God for enabling one to have reached a special time or place.

There is nothing so special as the Sabbath with all her traditions, songs, and prayers, but none can compare with the one spent in Jerusalem at the Western Wall.

As I approached the Wall I felt the presence of generation upon generation of my forebears. I inserted my prayer in a fissure in the wall that held countless other prayers.

Marcia Rome Levitz

A Sabbath Blessing

She comes to us so silently
As the sun sets o'er the Western Wall.
While voices loudly sing Her praises,
She brings hope of Peace to all.
She warms the children's faces
In the glow of candlelight.
She delights in mankind's respite
From his toils and his strife,
And she teaches that the spirit
Is renewed when we bless His name.
We bless His name forever
As we light the Sabbath flames.

Massada

The trek up Massada started early the next morning. There is something quite unique in your sense of accomplishment when you finally reach the top. This had been King Herod's summer palace and the final resting place for nine hundred and fifty Jewish men, women, and children.

The hike along the Snake Trail links your past to the present as you place one foot in front of the other ascending the worn rocky steps. There was an excitement in the arid hot air-and I do mean hot! We were told at the end of the day that the temperature had reached 130-degree Farenheit, but like the zealots of old, we were not deterred from achieving our goal.

Groups of fellow climbers rested, drank water, and kibitzed at various lookout points, but an inner drive pushed us all forward and upward, linking us together in a chain of friendship and camaraderie.

King Herod's summer palace, at Massada, an ancient fortress town located in southeast Israel west of the Dead Sea, was the last stronghold of the zealots. More than nine hundred Jews escaped slavery in Jerusalem and held off the Romans for two years, watching the death ramp being built by their brethren who had been enslaved. These zealots believed that they were the last remnants of the Jewish faith. They fought for their freedom, and they died together in a mass suicide lest they, too, be enslaved. According to historians, there were

Marcia Rome Levitz

10,000 enslaved Jews employed to build this death ramp.

Under a floor tile in the assembly area of the palace the zealots left biblical quotations, indicating their hope that from their dead bones would spring forth a new generation of believers-and so it was, and so it is.

We Jews have survived a multitude of persecutions. My hot and exhausting travail up Massada was but an inconsequential test compared to what others have endured and are still enduring, but it made me feel that I followed in their footsteps, and it makes me hope to create my own footsteps for others to follow.

Among Red Poppies In The Sand

The Romans in the second revolt
Laid waste to the land,
Tore man from wife,
Destroyed all life.
The land was afire,
But the desire for freedom
Would not expire.

The land once fertile and green with life,
Lay desolate, eroding,
A swamp of despair;
Yet it yearned to bear
The olive, the orange, the fig, and the pear
In isolated pockets of toil and care.

It's April now, and the fragrant flowers
Spring forth upon their wind-blown boughs.
With a scent so sweet on the gentle breeze
That barbed-wired borders cannot prevent
The passing of their promise.
"We shan't fall again," and shan't forget.

Marcia Rome Levitz

A Child Is A Blessing

I am blessed with a handsome, self-assured son who brings me joy everyday, and yet I always yearned to have a daughter. I now feel as though I have six hundred daughters because I visited a Jewish girls orphanage on Saturday, our day of rest.

Among Red Poppies In The Sand

A child is born into this world
To family, and yet I found her here,
In an orphanage for girls.

A safer haven than she once had,
In donated skirt and blouse she was clad;
And in her room so simple, so neat,
A pair of shoes beside her feet.

From a prayer book she did read aloud
And glanced but once at the door to see
Who stood there, oh, so proud.

I walked on through the empty halls
These girls would call their home,
Until they married and moved on
To families of their own.

Six hundred girls this family strong;
They are our future,
To each of us they should belong.

Marcia Rome Levitz

Eretz Israel

The ten days I spent in Israel both fulfilled and exhausted me emotionally. One particularly difficult day was Yom Ha'zika'ron, the day of national mourning. That day on Mount Herzl, the resting place for thousands of Israel's defenders, we mourned. Not only did we mourn for the six million who died in the Holocaust, but also for the young men and women who have given their lives since 1948 in support of Israel's right to exist and the innocents caught in the crossfire. We still mourn.

I witnessed mothers, sisters, and brothers, some uniformed, honoring the memory of fallen soldiers, aged sixteen, seventeen, eighteen, and nineteen, with fresh bouquets of flowers on grave after grave. Grief overwhelmed each of us there, and yet a sense of national unity pervaded the atmosphere. We shared the common knowledge that without their sacrifice we might not be able to stand here together.

There were Jews from the world over: some visiting as were we, some who had made alliyah, the Russians here so briefly, the Ethiopians and the Moroccans striving to learn Hebrew, and the newly arrived Mexican with whom I spoke who was trying to make it on his own in the face of "no room at the inn," and the Sabra whose family in the past fifty-two years had made Israel the 8th wonder of the world.

Israel is a melting pot of Jewish cultures. We have been forced over the centuries into the Diaspora. Having a homeland enable us as Jews to identify and honor our heritage. Ignoring politics and religion, this region belongs to all of us.

Evening comes with a siren loud.
Remembering all who served her proud.
Eretz Israel, your people shan't forget.
To you we
Zionists pledge, for with you our future's set.

It's the feeling in your heart, from the
Start when you first see, a
Red sunset spread its warming glow
Atop the hills of Galilee.
Evening comes and at His request;
Let the Sabbath spirit bring Peace and rest.

Awakening

In my poems I have tried to capture the essence of what this mission has meant to me. I was always disturbed by friends who came back from Israel and said they could not explain the experience...that one must go to Israel to appreciate fully the history and the homage to this hallowed arena of diverse religions. We should be striving for cooperation and understanding of each other's values at his crucial time in our history. This is a fact; for those who have been to Israel, you know what I am talking about. For those who have not been to Israel, you must go and see for yourselves. She touches your heart in such a profound way that nothing else will ever impress you as She does. Once you go there, you will want to go again.

Regardless of our individual religious beliefs, Israel is a spiritual home for all.

I call this poem "Awakening." It has many meanings, both literal and figurative, which I feel capture my emotional ties with our land; Eretz Israel!

Among Red Poppies In The Sand

It's long before the sun will rise,
But sleep has left these tired eyes
That now are filled with tears for you.

My heart does ache to return to you,
The Promise Land,
For the bonds made there
Left my life renewed.

Together we share a common past,
The future will bring peace at last,
To all who mourn-who hold life dear.

There are those who want the spirit to die,
Who have no heart, no tear in their eye,
Who think of life as something to fear.

With outstretched arms I reach for you,
Embrace the warmth of love so new,
And yet I knew it was always there.

Like a spark of life seen in an eye,
That weeps for children that had to die,
Who at Yad Layeled light the sky.
There's no more time to wonder why.
It's time to show the world we care.

Marcia Rome Levitz

What I Know Now

Inside my chest there beats a heart,
That like the waters that Moses did part,
For my people, it too, is breaking apart,

It bleeds like a plaque sent from God above,
Who showed to Noah the turtle dove,
And who in His goodness showed us love.

My words spill out upon this page
As I write of this world in a brand new age.
Am I alone in this rage?

The time has come for humankind
To reach inside-try to define
Their reasons for staying mute and blind.

I know not much of this world of ours,
The politics, the pathos,
The loss of our two towers.
One thing I know: God's love is power.

Epilogue

Nothing could have prepared us
For what occurred on September 11, 2001,
But holding onto the precepts
That love of God, self, and humankind,
Regardless of religious beliefs,
We as a world united
Shall find the peace and harmony
We all were promised.
Let us find ourselves counted

Among Red Poppies in the Sand.

I traveled to Israel again in 1991 and took my son there for his Bar Mitzvah gift. I also took some classes in the evening and had my own Bat Mitzvah at the top of Massada; as I hadn't had the chance as a young girl. At my time, age 13, Rabbis were not allowing girls to become Bat Mitzvah. I shall cherish that experience forever.

I would love to go back again so another trip is on my bucket list.

www.ingramcontent.com/pod-product-compliance
Ingram Content Group UK Ltd.
Pitfield, Milton Keynes, MK11 3LW, UK
UKHW020244240426
12048UKWH00026B/1601